The Tao of
S E X

An Erotic Bedside Companion

Nell Gwyn

DRRTY GRRL PRODUCTIONS

The Tao of Naughty series is presented by:

Drrty Grrl Productions

Erotic Exploration & Empowerment

Many movements converge in

the symphony of sex.

You will want for nothing.

who needs cookies?

Sex is to the body as

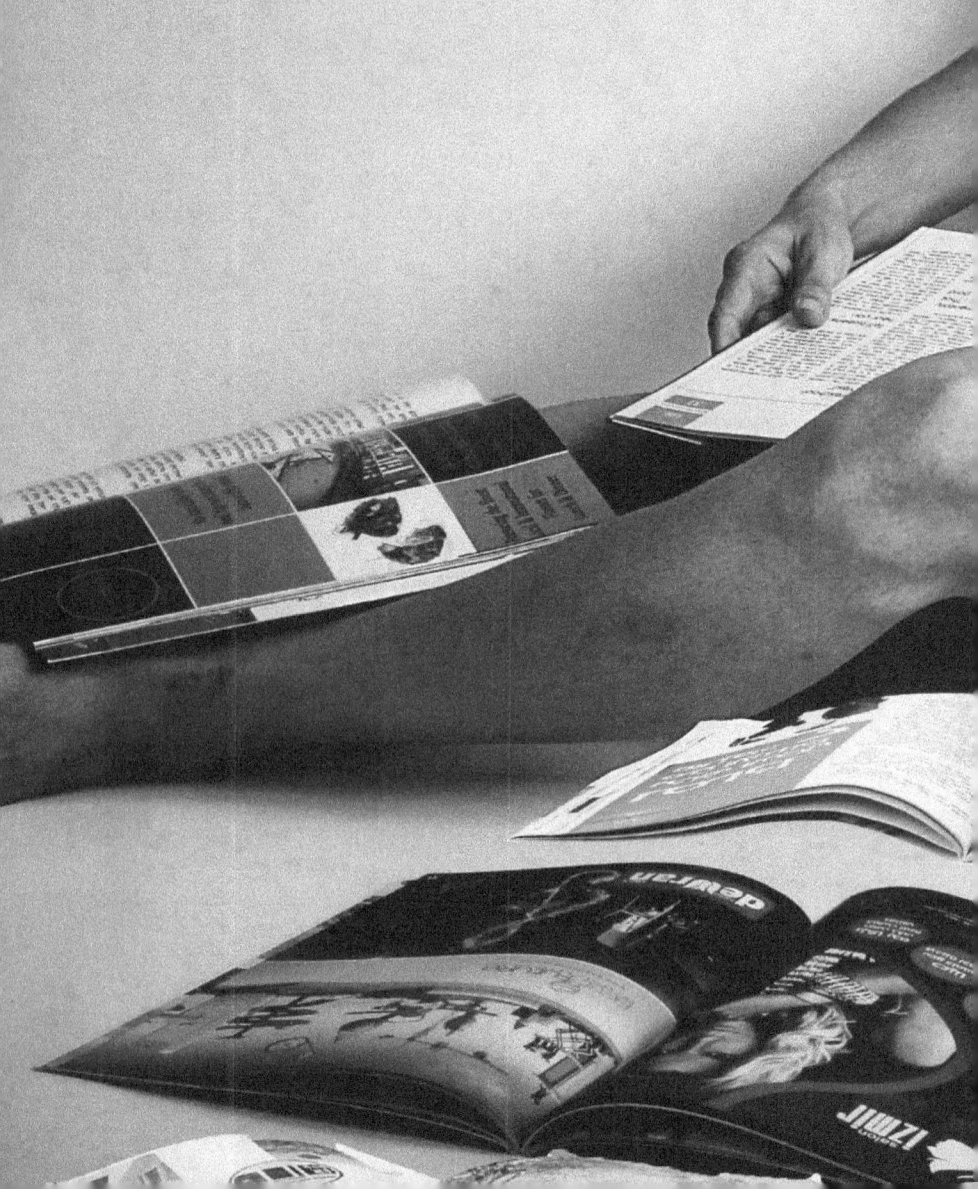

no room for guilt.

Monogamy has

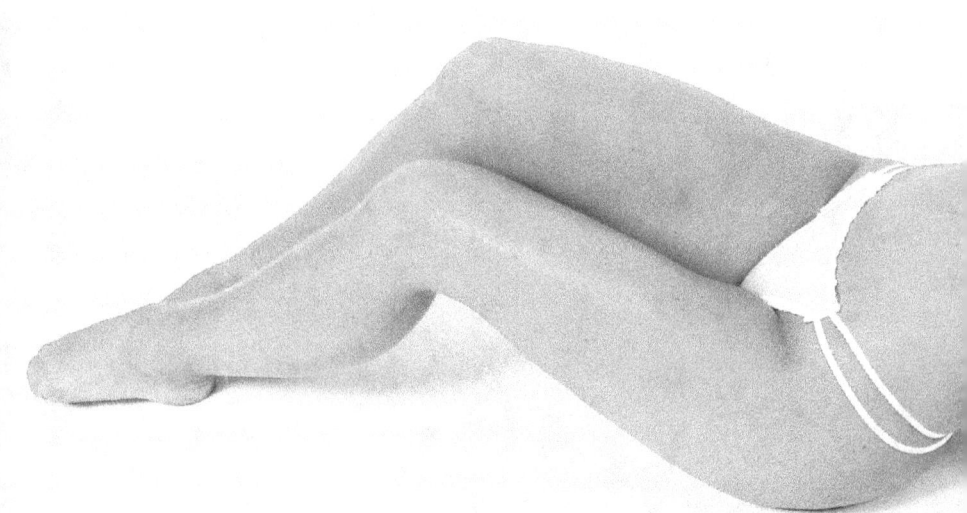

die of pleasure.

Size matters

Feed a lover's needs

to satiate your own.

Never hesitate to

do the job yourself.

Love is all good.

Aware sex is fabulous.

What, or who, are you

Respect your partner

to respect yourself.

those who listen.

Bedtime is

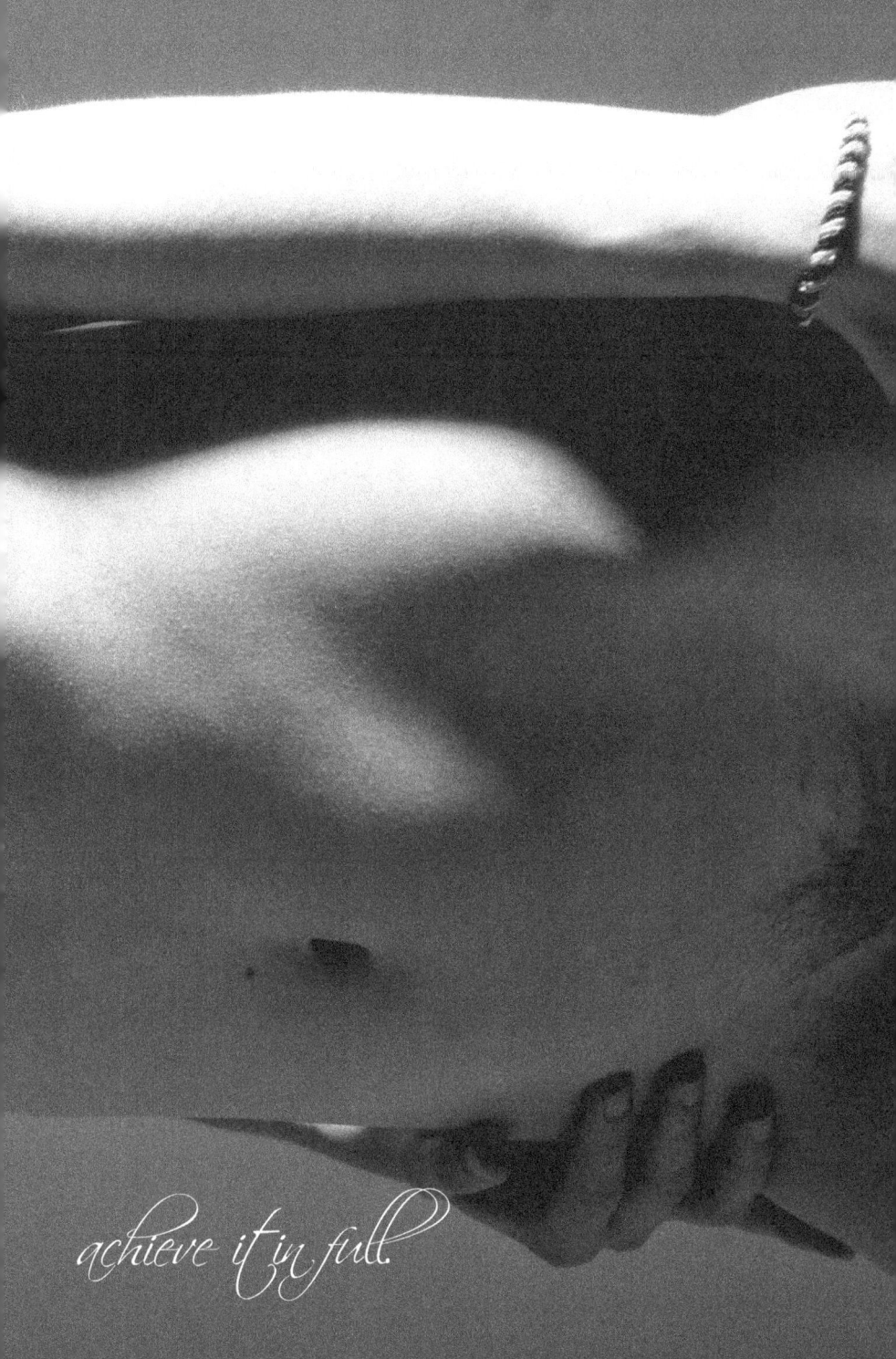

Being ravished

Total engagement springs

from total abandon.

Role-playing offers

The language of love has

Even if it's not fabulous,

it can still be fun.

refreshes and revives.

Tantric mastery

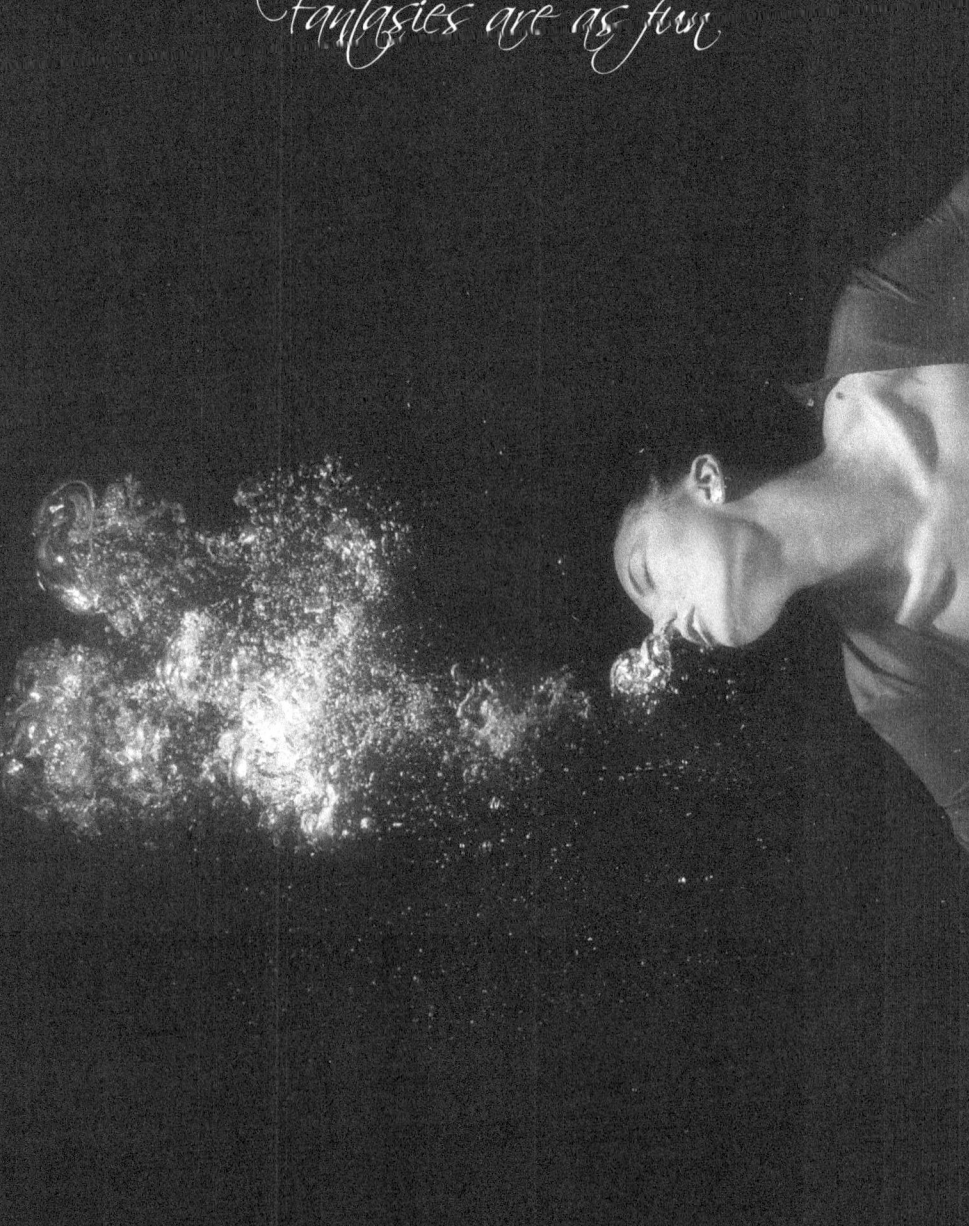
Fantasies are as fun

as realities.

Mechanics are enhanced

by motives.

Touch is

transcendent.

the flames of passion

consume all

Quantity is less important

shaking the body

shivers the soul.

An inch of skin is a

broad erotic field.

How it looks stimulates.

How it feels culminates.

A fetish

Stop or go.

The mind is the most

A little creativity

Naughty is as

naughty does.

between those who love.

The Tao of Naughty Series

The Tao of Sex
An Erotic Bedside Companion

The Tao of Bondage
An Erotic BDSM Companion

The Tao of BDSM
An Erotic Playtime Companion

www.ingramcontent.com/pod-product-compliance
Lightning Source LLC
Chambersburg PA
CBHW060042230426
43661CB00004B/629